Chocolate Love Letters

Also by Toni Cole "Negro Woman"

© 2010

Chocolate Love Letters

For Black Men from the Women & Children Who Love Them

Written by TONI COLE

First published June 2016

Copyright © 2016, Toni Cole.

ISBN-13: 978-692-73730-9

ISBN-10: 0-692-73730-8

Printed in the United States of America.

This book is dedicated to black men and boys who have been victims of mass incarceration, police brutality and senseless acts of gun violence.

I called upon the LORD in distress; the LORD
answered me, and set me in a large place.

The LORD is on my side; I will not fear: what can
man do unto me?

The LORD taketh my part with them that help me:
therefore, shall I see my desire upon them that hate
me.
It is better to trust in the LORD than to put
confidence in man.

Psalm 118: 5-8

<u>Introduction</u>

Chocolate Love Letters gives you an intimate look into the resilience of love shared within the black family.

<u>Contents</u>

Chapter 1

The Struggle is Real

A MAN DEFERRED

What happens to a man deferred?
Does he implode and wither away? Or explode one day?
Does he vanish in racism's thirsty flame?
Dismissed in the history books' altered pages?

What happens to the psyche of a black man?
Our fathers, husbands, sons, brothers, uncles, cousins and
nephews
Whose blood is splattered all over the daily news
Brains oozing in the street like rotted meat?

America's most hated. Public Enemy #1.
But who's got the gun?

Does he give into society's fears?
Becoming the beast so many fear?
Or is his life spent
Trying to make those who hate him believe?

Believe that he's different
Educated and nobody's fool
He must learn
That it's his color, his color, the color of his skin
That sweet dark-ebony hue
That has made him a marked man.

Are all black men doomed?
Yes! If we rely on researchers
And their altered statistics.

Generation after generation
The black man returns
Exotic black roses in full bloom
Amidst jagged slabs of concrete.

A man who refuses to be invisible
Flashing his locks as he arises from troubled waters
Naked, glistening and erect.
There he stands flat-footed,
Eye to eye and toe to toe with hate,
Determined to live another day.

Dear Daddy,

I never had a daddy. Mommy said you left before we had the chance to meet. So now it's just Mommy and me all the time. Christmas, Easter, Thanksgiving, Halloween, my birthdays and school plays. Mommy is the one who I run to when people mess with me. But my friend at school, she tells her daddy because he is tall with big hands. Daddy do you have big hands? Mommy's hands are small. She can't fix my bike, carry me on her shoulders or throw a ball very far. She rubs my bruises after a fall though, and her hugs are my favorite. She squeezes me so tight and doesn't want to let me go. Daddy do you have good hugs like mommy?

Daddy, I'm getting ready for junior high school and Mommy told me that I have to learn to catch the bus by myself. I'm scared! Why can't I be like other kids who call their dad when their mother can't pick them up from school? Daddy, do you have a cell phone? Guess what, Daddy? My aunt is taking me to the amusement park next week. I got good grades and that's my reward. Daddy would you be proud of me too? Mommy told me that I'm supposed to do well in school and not to expect a gift every time I get good grades.

I like gifts. I like having fun and laughing too. But, I don't like it when I see Mommy cry. I asked her why she cries and she said that's what people do when they're sad. Daddy, do you know why Mommy gets sad? I like French fries, reading books and Halo's.

Continued…

Last summer I read 10 books daddy. My class had a trip to the library and we all got our own library card. I love books! Daddy, do you love me?

Ok, Daddy I have to go to bed now. I'm going to put this letter in the shoebox under my bed where I keep all your letters. When Mommy buys me boots I'll use that box for letters because it holds more. Mommy said I couldn't mail them to you because she doesn't know where you live. Daddy, are you still alive? Ok, it's time for me to pray and ask God to watch over you and Mommy. Daddy, who will watch over me? Ok, good night, Daddy.

I Love You Daddy,

Baby Girl

Husband,

We need to get our act together! We both have gained so much weight since we've been married that we barely look like our former selves. Is our weight a sign that we're happy or unhappy? I mean with our lives. We need to change our behavior patterns if we plan on being around for a while.

I want to be healthy. I want us to be healthy! We just have to make up our minds to change what we eat and how much. The three horsemen: diabetes, high blood pressure, and cancer are taking our people out. We see it all around us, family members and friends who have to inject themselves with insulin, take pills to get up then more pills to go to sleep. That's not the life that I want for us.

Let's start by changing the way we prepare our food. I'll bake more and fry less. We can start loading up on fruits, veggies, nuts, seeds, grains so that we prepare nutritious foods. Also, the soda's got to go! We could purchase some really tasty sparkling waters with zero calories. We could even take an after dinner walk with the kids. Let's do this!

For Life,

Your Wife

Brothers,

I need to have a conversation with you about a subject that has bothered me for some time. Why is it that, some of you, berate black women when you're asked why you date outside your race? I often hear comments like, "Black women are angry, they're too bossy or they don't know how to treat a man." Then there are some of you who accuse black women of not taking care of themselves, which, when translated, oftentimes mean they don't measure up to the Western standard of beauty.

So who was it that made sure food was on the table when you couldn't find work? Were black women okay when you made blue collar money? Okay enough to bear your babies and raise your babies while you ran the streets? It was the black woman who traveled out of state to visit you in prisons and made sure you had money in your account and answered all those damn collect calls. Whose address did you use so that you could meet your pre-lease conditions? Who accepted you back over and over after your affairs?

Tell me…who prayed for you when you went away to college and sustained injuries while playing professional sports? Is your black momma the only black woman you love? I get that love is a beautiful gift that goes beyond the boundaries of color.

Continued...

But why is it that you have to justify your love for women outside your race by demonizing black women? Do what you do with courage.

Please, brother, open your eyes! See that when you turn your backs on black women you are turning your backs on your black mothers, aunties, sisters, nieces and friends. It hurts us knowing how we've shouldered your burdens but somehow are not good enough to walk by your side when you "make" it. Beware of any dream that forces you to denounce who you are and where you came from.

Real Talk.

Bro,

I've done just about every damn thing imaginable to stay with you. I compromised my integrity and became a shell of myself as I tried to "make" you happy. Happy yet? Or do you see my love as a pitiful plea made by a broken little bird? I was warned not to ask questions that I already knew the answer to. Shit! Desperate times call for desperate actions. Who do you share your beautiful smile with? Where did that spark in your eyes go? How did we get here?

I'm not stupid and I'm nobody's fool! I know you've been having an affair for quite some time now. All I want to do is take the little dignity I have left and piece my life back together. Praying that I never make the same mistake of forgetting my own happiness.

(Circa 2016)

…And One More Thing

I see you! You're the kind of man who's looking for a woman to take care of him. You'll give just enough of yourself to have us wanting more only to learn that there was nothing left. You are the sum total of your lack of goals, limited resources, one minute orgasms, and half a paycheck! Some women say that they'd rather do badly by themselves than to have someone like you around. Well, I was doing just fine before you showed up. Where did you come from anyway?

Tell me, what is it with guys like you? Were you missing in action during role identification training? You know when men were taught to protect and provide for their women and children. When lessons were taught about going to work every day and protecting the family, when men were taught how to be men.

Brothers like you make it bad for men who are out there holding it down. Even sadder is the women who put up with your foolishness! I blame them too. Get your shit together! Your woman, your kids and your community demand it of you!

(Circa 2016)

Dear Superman,

I need a hero! Will you rescue me in a single bound? Will you cover me with your wings of courage and make me feel delicate again? Will you allow me to be a damsel in distress, I mean literally fall to pieces without worry of being trampled upon or used? Can I tell you my secrets in the still of our nights? Will you be my Superman and have my back, my sides, my top and my bottom?

Hell! You want me to be Superwoman and do things that I wasn't made to do alone. Like…raise the kids, work full time, keep house and bring half to the table. Not to mention the freak you want in the bed and the lady in the street. I feel bipolar with your roller coaster of expectations. Somehow I feel you're taking me for a ride, yet I still try my best to hang on for it. I can only be me and if that's not enough spontaneity and excitement for you then go find it! Superwoman doesn't really exist unless she too wraps her head in a scarf at night and wear those ugly period panties to bed. The fire didn't go out in our relationship. Having unlimited access to a thing causes one to tire of it and take it for granted. That's just human nature. Don't let your immaturity throw away our good thing.

Love,

~~Super~~ Woman

My Love,

I just want to acknowledge your grief. Not only did I lose my baby… we lost *our* baby. I don't think people deliberately dote on me to ignore you. I've been with you long enough to know when you are hurting and this loss right here has broken your heart in two.

We've been told that we have what it takes to get through this storm but I sometimes wonder. I've seen your legs buckle from the pain as you held onto the bathroom sink to keep from going into a free fall. In those times I had to hold you in my strength, praying that one day this would somehow make sense. When you told me that you were angry with God…I got it! We did everything right, we got married, we saved, we bought a home to raise our children in. We even planned the first birthday party. Damn it! Why our baby? Why us?

In Grief,

Your Help-Meet

Dear Husband,

When I catch you watching me, it makes me wonder if I've lost something that you still need. Tell me, because if I need to make some changes I will. Is it too late? Even the compliments you once showered upon me dissipated. That sparkle...my sparkle...in your eyes dimmed one night. I must say your swag has been on fleek as of late. Every week you come home with another bottle of expensive cologne, you're in the gym four nights a week, and now you're drinking all those protein shakes instead of my home cooked meals.

You're so agreeable we don't argue anymore. Is it still good to you?

Husband, I know there's another woman in your life. In fact, I can guess the time frame you started messing around on me. Would it happen to have been a couple of months back when you came home with flowers professing your love for me? You remember the night when you cooked dinner, washed the dishes and took out the trash!

Is she everything you wished for? Does she, this woman, this other woman have you wishing you were single again? I tell you what...I'm not going to compete for something that I thought was already mine. I've given you my heart inside and out to make sure you had it all. I have nothing left to give...you.

Continued…

Husband I'll give you a few days to think about what you want to do. But you cannot have it both ways. You already know I don't play seconds. The clock is ticking.

Waiting,

Your Wife!

Really?

All I can say is wow! I was really having a good time getting to know you before the wall popped up between us. I'm not sure what happened, I thought we had great chemistry. What happened? How did you go from calling me daily to not answering my calls? I've even texted you long messages as much as I hate doing that. When I ran into you the other day at the coffee bar you acted as if there was never an "us." Remember the time you asked me why I seemed so guarded and distrustful? Well, this is a prime example of why I take my time with guys because in the beginning it's all smoke and mirrors! I've learned that only time can reveal the truth about someone. But I must say that I enjoyed you! As short lived as "it" was. Peace!

From,

A Grown Ass Woman

Dear Brothers,

Let me be clear. What you label "angry black women" is actually women who are fighting for their lives. Women who are drowning, hurting and left alone to fend for themselves without the comfort and protection of their men. You talk about the "issues" we have but do nothing to help resolve them. On the opposite end of that spectrum is the brothers who proudly boast of the "strong black women" in their lives. As if raising a family alone and working two jobs just to put food on the table is an attribute to be pursued. We don't get to walk away from our lives yet, men do it every day.

Brothers seem to forget that before a woman became a wife and mother she was She. Not a play-thing, freak, bitch, thot or any of the other unspeakable names you comfortably ascribe to us. How do you expect other people to respect you when you treat your women in such a way?

From,

Overwhelmed & Hurting

Brother,

Look here, I know you're used to women waiting on you hand and foot, including your momma, but I don't play house. I'm too grown for that. Yes, you have to leave at a decent hour. You can't spend three nights out of the week at my house—that's too much like shacking. I don't need you to pay my bills, but I can always use a few extra dollars. Now if you want to cut the grass or fix a pipe from time to time, help yourself. I've grown accustomed to a certain lifestyle that I have no intention of compromising to make you feel less threatened.

I prefer to keep my financial business to myself so please don't start hinting about how much money I make. All you need to know is that I make enough to take care of myself. I'm not a gold digger. However, I do like a nice surprise every so often.

Time will let me know if you're the right one for me. I'm looking for a man who adores me. I want him to love my heart, my smile, my skin, my hair and all my peculiarities. I want to know that I can call on him without hearing a whole lot of excuses and reasons why he can't be there. I believe that when a relationship starts with a story it ends with a story. So if you're looking for me to take care of you it's about five years too late.

From,

40 plus

Hey Man,

Look, don't expect me to run into your arms and tell you how much I missed you. Man, you fucked up! You abandoned us and left my mother to care for me and my little sisters. She had to work around the clock, with little sleep in between, and still fell short making ends meet. I wasn't going to watch my mom's work herself to death so I had to become the man of the house. A real man take care of his responsibilities and that's what I did. I'm the one who made sure we ate and had lights and heat. You can say what you want but I did what I had to do in those streets. It is what it is! I got dudes out there that will take a bullet for me and we not even related. When I stand over my homie's caskets, I stand alone, with more questions than answers. Here I supposed to be your fucking son and you haven't done shit for me. For real, you dead to me. As far as I'm concerned you fucked up and ain't no coming back from that. If you really want to step up and show that you're a changed man, then be there for my little sisters while they still give a fuck!

My Mother's Son.

My Friend,

Let's talk about a subject that is still taboo. How difficult it must have been for you to come out of the "closet." But, in the light of courage you said, "I am a gay man." Wow! Knowing that there would be people waiting to marginalize, judge and even hate you. Despite it all, you did it anyway. As much progress as this country seemed to have made around the subject, do you believe there are still packed closets bolted shut? I ask because there's always news of someone who committed suicide for being outed. How awful it must be to have your love handcuffed. To be a man of color is one thing but to be a gay man of color has to be all the more difficult.

I want you to know that I love you and appreciate your courage. Go back and gather your broken pieces. Gently piece them together until you're able to recognize yourself again. Inhale love and exhale hate. There are still people in this world whose love is unconditional. People who know that God is LOVE.

In Admiration.

Chapter 2

Rise!

I CAN BREATHE

Barely, as racism tightens its noose around my neck
A psychotic rage incapable of seeing my humanity
My decency
ME

I can breathe!
This thick air of civil disobedience
As black people tire
From injustice
Left with no choice but to resist

I can breathe!
And as long as I'm alive
I will shout about
Tender black trees falling
And their ghostly screams

I can breathe!
No! Hatred won't cut off my air supply
My ancestors left an endless supply of strength
The welts on their backs left a decree
"Love liberty more than you fear death"

Dearest Brothers,

Jail ain't home! It can't bake you cornbread in a cast iron skillet and homemade birthday cakes with your name written in chocolate frosting. It won't allow you to be there for your children ensuring that they master new skills. It doesn't offer you the opportunity to tuck your kids in bed and kiss them before turning out the lights. Jail doesn't have carpet on the floors and pretty pictures on the wall. It doesn't offer unobstructed views. You don't get to make love to your love early in the morning before breakfast. The inmates are not really your family; they don't have your DNA.

Home is home! Where your family is waiting for your return. Your absence has left a hole where creepy crawling things are setting up shop. The family is doing the best they can but how much better it would be if you were here. Your children miss you...not the man they see in that tan onesie once a month, for one hour. They miss your presence, your guidance, your protection, your essence, your heart, your smile, your humor, your manhood. They miss Daddy!

Jail ain't home! I don't care how many times you return. I don't give a damn how many programs they offer. To hell with its boasts of rehabilitation. Jail is a cage and as with all cages you are forbidden to fly.

Continued…

When they unlock the cage this time, see jail for what it is: a time stealer, a home wrecker, an identity eraser, a *big business* with you as the collateral. A money making machine. The antithesis of home.

Love,
Your Tribe

To Our Tender Fallen Trees,

I'm so sorry that no one was there to protect you …to save you. I'm so sorry that you were run down and left alone in the company of unbridled hatred. When I think of the fear you must have felt unarmed crying for mercy, the mother inside of me rise up and screams, "Somebody help my baby...somebody!" I can't wrap my head around the fact that you are no longer with us. Your death was senseless! We failed you…America and its judicial system. Yet somehow, even in your death, you were found guilty and deserving of your fate. God help us!

A war has been waged against you and all the trees that look like you. It's an ongoing war that was waged ever since our peoples arrived on these here shores. We as a people know that the terrorists within are equally as dangerous as those without. Black boys and men have been hung from trees, shot down and economically castrated for years.

The assassin's bullet tried to rob the world of your unique contributions. Yet all over the country people of all nationalities and races are standing in unification to proclaim that Black Lives Matter! They get it! They are beginning to understand what Dr. Martin Luther King, Jr. meant when he said that injustice anywhere is a threat to injustice everywhere. May Your Legacy Live On Forever.

The Village

Homie,

I heard your boy was murdered the other day. I'm so sorry because I know how close you two were. In fact, you called him your brother. You guys were always together, when you saw one you saw the other. He had your back and you had his. Someone said that you were blaming yourself for not being there the night he was killed. Death is strange in that way; it manages to creep in during hours unaware.

It's almost déjà vu. What was it a year ago—another brother in the neighborhood was gunned down on that same corner? This crazy world challenges even the strongest among us. Try to find comfort in the fact that your friend knew you loved him. There was nothing you could have done to prevent what took place.

I'm not going to tell you to be strong because you are. I'm not going to tell you to hold your head up because you keep it up. Just know that you are not alone during this difficult time. Just as you had your boy's back…I've got yours.

Till Death!

Dear Nephew,

Congratulations on your wedding day! I wish you all the happiness your heart can hold. I can't think of anyone more deserving than you. You've been through so much drama with past relationships, but I watched you maintain your dignity through it all. Not once did you raise your hand to those women or disrespect them in any way. When your last relationship ended because of her affair, you walked away holding your heart in your hands. Through it all you managed to finish school with honors and now have a wonderful career.

I hear some of the comments made by haters who don't know your story. That's how you know their spirit, they don't care to know. I know you've heard them as well, but you didn't let them distract you from reaching your goals or from following your dreams. I am so proud of you! You've been accused of forgetting where you came from. The next time tell them you didn't forget, you just don't want to go back there.

Love,

Auntie

Young Man,

There are some things you must now understand because I can't have you going out into the world ignorant. It could mean life or death for you. There are so many possibilities before you. Today you can go into any profession of your choosing, creating the life that was impossible not too long ago for people of color. You need to know your history and the cloth that you're made from. You come from a strong people. A people who have been enslaved, marginalized and murdered yet continue to rise. Black men, especially, have it difficult for reasons too numerous to name but hate is at the core of them all.

Most blacks in America were brought here as slaves, stolen from their native lands of Africa and the Caribbean. We were used for free labor. Which means we did all the work while others got wealthy off our backs. As slaves we were considered chattel (animals) only two-thirds of a human being according to the Constitution of the United States. Because slaves were looked upon as something other than human it was permissible for them to be lynched, burned, sold, whipped, raped, and suffer the unspeakable. Man's humanity towards man! Never forget your history because history has a way of repeating itself. Remember to remember!

Continued...

Today, black boys and men are shot down in the streets like dogs sometimes for no reason at all. The "Saboteur" of your ancestors is still on the rampage.

My hope is that you read this and walk towards your dreams mindful of who you are and where you come from. You come from a praying people so don't ever neglect the ritual of prayer because if God is for you- *no one* can be against you. Look to God for help, for protection and guidance. Live free! Despite the ominous clink of the chains that thirst for your bondage. Duck and dodge, whatever you have to do to avoid the gaping hole that wants to bury you alive. Thrive! Then pass your wisdom and strength on to other young black men. Be your brother's keeper, shield him from the traps that are constantly devised for his capture.

From,

The Elders

To My Hero,

I tried to finish this book earlier but there were unforeseen distractions which prevented that from happening or so I thought. Then it occurred to me that I had not included you in this book...my book to black men. The same divine Love that placed us in each other's lives ensured that I took advantage of this opportunity to write a letter expressing just how much you mean to me.

Scofield, you've poured so much of your wisdom and strength into me, I am the woman I am today because of you. I've fearlessly shared my heart and soul with you. It still amazes me how much alike we are, you get me! There hasn't been a time when I needed you and you were not there. There were times I wished you were my father but, had you been my father I might not have been as receptive to your guidance.

Scofield, you knew me before I knew myself. You saw my potential when I was still cowering before the woman in the mirror. When I shared my lofty dreams you assured me that I could always make another decision if things didn't go as I had planned. Whenever I accomplished a goal you were there cheering me on, "Go Toni, Go Toni!"

Chocolate Love Letters

Continued…

Scofield, you've taught me how to thank God for EVERYTHING. You cautioned me that we all had a price to pay for being human but, as long as I relied on God I would be safe and secure.

When I went through a divorce you were there. When I met the man who I "thought" was my father you were there to help me make sense of it all. When I discovered, some years later, that man was not my father you helped me back from the brink of despair.

Scofield, you've been my mentor and friend for many years. Anyone who knows me, knows just how much you mean to me. Thank you for everything!

Love,
Toni

Black Man,

I'm not sure if you know how bad things are with the relationship between the black man and woman. Here we are beautiful, successful and without the comforts of a man. What happened? You used to court us, pursue us and do what was necessary to be with us. In some weird way our roles reversed. Women now pursue you! And what's even more pathetic is that you let them. You've grown accustomed to women taking you out to dinner, paying for your manicures and pedicures and showering you with gifts. As you exploit our innate desire for your touch and need to feel like women again.

It's now fashionable for you to let women know that you have a "situation" as if that clears your conscience of the damage you have planned for the women involved. Some of you are so blunt that you've taken to introducing your love interests to one another. What happened to your heart?

Then you call us all kinds of bitches and hoes with the same hatred used when someone calls you a nigga. You'll watch us struggling with our bags and won't lift a finger to help us. Instead of making our lives easier you expect for us to take care of you. Then get mad when we say that we're "open" to dating outside our race.

Continued...

Is this dis-connect the result of years of racism and systematic isms that have caused us to eat our own?

Black men...tell us what to do. Your women need the King in you to rise up.

Our children need to feel safe again. Our home needs your blessing so that it can be a refuge. The place where we seduce one another. A sacred space for truth and knowledge.

If you're a King, I speak blessings to you and the Queen by your side.

Peace & Blessings!

Dear Son,

Thank you for your service to this country. At first I didn't want to let you go until you told me that freedom wasn't free. You've sacrificed so much for this country. But you left my baby boy and came back a man, just look at you! I'm so proud of you. The family is proud of you.

You've set a fine example for your younger brothers, cousins and nephews. Take advantage of the opportunities that are afforded you for serving this country honorably.

Love,

Mother

Dearest Brothers,

It must be painful knowing that you are the MOST HATED man in America! To be marginalized, labeled a street thug who only sells drugs and goes to prison. Like how do you keep a smile on your face and show up for life everyday knowing that lurking around every corner is someone else's fears, someone ready to destroy you? What do you think when you turn on the news and see images of yourself murdered in the street surrounded by thirsty bloodhounds and bystanders? How does it make you feel when you see the prisons system's orgasmic urgency to make more cells...for you?

Brother talk to me! Are you afraid of dying when you've never fully lived? Have you given up completely on the so-called American Dream? If so, what then moves you and makes you feel alive? What do you have hope in? Who brings you joy?

Brother, just know that I love you and I'm not afraid to say it! I think you're beautiful in the most profound way. Your history makes you beautiful, your body is beautiful. Your mind and tenacity are beautiful. Your smile is beautiful. The way you dance, rap, hoop, catch, swing, sing, beat the drum and tap your way through life is beautiful. Your swag is beautiful. Brothers, you are our lions walking against the wind.

Continued...

Keep walking...never stop walking. Dance hard. Fuck hard. Play hard. Love hard and stay hard as we walk through this valley together.

From,

Sisters in the Struggle

Dear Uncle Sunny,

You were the only uncle I've ever known and I loved you so much! I still think of the crazy stuff we used to do. You had a knack for getting in trouble. You had a heart of gold but, like so many others you gave away so much.

As a little girl I'd hear people say, "That Sunny is a mess!" or "You know he's a faggot!?" I never liked that word because it rhymed with maggot. You reminded me of Prince. You were a very attractive man with a fair complexion, hazel eyes and black curly hair. You had beautiful white teeth and a little petite build yet was very strong. AIDS came like a thief in the night and took you away from me.

Even your longtime partner John fell victim to the diseases long reach. John was a gentle soul with a lot of patience to put up with your shenanigans for over 25 years. He made you a better person! I'll never forget our final night with John. He actually came to the family room, a space in the house that he didn't care much for. In silence he roamed the room with his eyes finally picking up every single knickknack from the fireplace mantel before leaving without a word.

I was with you when you got the call the next morning saying that John had passed away. I was shaken to the core by your groans and wailing. At the hospital, I watched you run to John, lifting him in your arms, rocking and kissing him as you called out to him in a tone that echoed into eternity.

Continued…

I remember very little about the day you told me that you too were infected. It was all a blur. There was the solo trip you took to the islands and some talk of a Last Will & Testament.

I still laugh when I think of that time we were grocery shopping and I asked you whether you had any Grey Poupon. In a sarcastic way you replied "No, but I have mustard."

You stayed on my back, always encouraging me to utilize my gifts and talents. Uncle Sunny, are you proud of me now? You lived your life out loud before it was acceptable to do so. You were courageous, smart and daring…traits that I've gotten from you.

I'll never forget the last time I saw you. You waved good bye to me from a hospital bed. Uncle Sunny, it's never goodbye, only see you later.

Out here on the West Coast I've met an amazing group of friends. Did you have something to do with our chance meeting? Thank you Uncle Sunny.

Missing You,

Toni

Young Man!

Have you lost your mind? What are you doing out here robbing, stealing and killing? Don't you have a conscience? What happened in you that you think it's okay to be cruel to folk? You weren't raised to be a menace to society. You should be out here making a contribution so that this world can be a better place for us all.

You've traded in books and knowledge for blunts and ignorance. You're so high you don't even know what's going on around you. Open your eyes! Open your eyes! Wake up and open your eyes! The ground is shifting beneath you. Don't you know that without a proper education and a skill set you won't get far in this life? There are people with degrees and work experience that have difficulty making a decent living, what do you think is in store for you?

What, you think it is a badge of honor to go to jail? If you do you reality will be grim. You will be punished for that crime a hundred times over. You'll have a stigma stuck to you for the rest of your life. If you think I'm lying talk to the folk who have been to jail and can't find work to make a decent living. Or to the men who still can't vote or get a student loan to pay for a college education.

You got your mother losing sleep worried that she's going to get called in the middle of the night that you've been killed out in those streets. That's the road you're walking down. It's time to make a detour.

Continued…

No one is going to be able to protect you once you get in that penal system. As much as your family done for you, look at how you repay us. You smoke dope, get drunk, abandon your babies and mistreat their mothers. Get your shit together!

Stop acting like a boy and be a man and if you don't know how then find a man that will teach you. At the end of the day you are responsible for your actions—good, bad or indifferent. I am not coming to see you trapped behind some bars like a caged animal. My heart can't take it. I am not going to throw you a party when you get out of jail, parties are for people who have accomplished something. Like returning from military service or college. I'm not going to accept this foolishness as a new normal. Even if that means I have to stand alone in holding your ass accountable. Enough is enough!

Big Momma

Hi Dad,

I have never met you before but I wanted to take this time to introduce myself to you. I am a good person that likes to have fun, dance, write poetry, and encourage people. Let me see…I am dark skinned with short hair and am told I have a beautiful smile. I figured I must look a lot like you because I bear little resemblance to my mother. I was a straight A student until I wasn't. But, I managed to get it together, eventually obtaining a Master's Degree and becoming a business woman. Oh! I'm an author as well. I think you would be proud of me.

Dad, I was married once but I'm not sure if I'm that girl. At the time I buckled to the pressure of what people expected of me rather than what I wanted for myself. You live and you learn, today I make my own decisions. Now that I think of it I was never the girl who dreamt of being married with kids. Rather, I imagined a fabulous life of world travel, exotic friends, and the resources to make that lifestyle possible. As you probably guessed I'm very independent, sometimes to a fault. It's just that I've had to learn the hard way to look out for number one.

Dad, I may never know what really happened between you and my mother. For all I know she may not have even told you that she was pregnant, I'll never know. What I do know is how it feels to be a fatherless child. Interesting, I'm a writer and still cannot find the words to express those feelings. All I have is the metaphor of a baby abandoned in the middle of a dark field in bleak of winter, that's it.

Continued…

Alright, let me get back to the business at hand. Understanding I may never meet you in this lifetime. Which also happens to mean that I am without your kin folk, a side of me that I will never know. Life!

Just Talking,

Toni

Pop,

There are so many young men who missed their rite of passage into manhood. The only markers for them were their ability to obtain a driver's license, legally purchase alcohol and make babies they weren't necessarily prepared to father. They were never celebrated for who they were and where they were headed. Yet society expected something from these men that they have yet to be taught. Sure, there's the respect these men received, from both women and men, for his sexual prowess. Which somehow is supposed to equate to manhood. But when it comes to the real conquest of our mind and flesh they often fall short.

Granddad, you gave me that rite of passage and I am so thankful. It wasn't a ritual that took place deep in the woods with drums beating, fire pits and a community of male elders. Instead it was a day trip with just the two of us where you shared a vulnerability you kept at bay until that moment. There wasn't a circumcision where my foreskin was removed yet you told me in no uncertain terms that it was time to put away childish things like indecision, promiscuity, poor money management and naiveté about life. You warned me to remember the ancestors' whose shoulders I stood on. You emphasized the courage and strength that was required for them to survive the atrocities of slavery and Jim Crow.

Continued…

Wow! All this time I looked at their submission as a weakness to never be repeated. And I said as much to you but before I could continue with my philosophical rant you interrupted me and told me that SURVIVAL was of the utmost importance to my ancestors. That it was in the surviving that generations to come would one day taste the freedom that eluded them. Granddad, thanks for my rite of passage into manhood.

Your Grandson

Dear Phillip:

What's going on big brother? I know it's been a while since I last dropped you a line but know that I am always thinking of you big brother. I wanted you to know that I finally published a book of poetry entitled "Negro Woman." I tried on two separate occasions to mail you an autographed copy of my book but it was returned to me. I cried! I really wanted you to know that your little sister's dream came true. All I could think of was the nights you and I would sit in my bedroom window looking up at the stars talking about what we wanted to be when we grew up. I always said I wanted to be a writer, remember?

What's going on with you? Did you put my name on the visiting list? When are visiting hours? Have you talked to your nieces lately? When are you coming home? The family is doing fine…you now have one great niece and four great nephews! Your oldest nephew is settling down nicely. Mom's getting older but she looks great. Oh, by the way I'm about to publish my second book entitled, "Chocolate Love Letters: For Black Men from the Women & Children Who Love Them." Big brother I had to do something to show the love that I have for you and all my brothers.

Love,

Toni

Chapter 3

Our Love

ALWAYS THERE

There was you
Right there
At all times
Always on time

I didn't have to call for you
Dream of you
Because when I reached out
There you were

Oh, what comfort
What joy
What love
Yes, it was
It is your love
That teaches me how to love

Not just that which is comfortable
But even the unknown
With all of its horror

I can walk through the bleakness of life
Pissed pants and all
Until I stand in the warmth
Of your love once more

No mountain is too high
No valley too low
No dream impossible
In the light of your love
All that is becomes love

Darling,

I love your dirty draws! I know some will call me crazy and say all sorts of things about me. But they don't know how good you make me feel. When I come home after a long day of work with all sorts of stuff on my mind, you still know how to get my attention and make me relax. Whether by rubbing my feet, massaging my neck or brushing my hair. Your touch alone is good for all that ails me. You are my dark knight, the one who gives me good loving. I mean, you bring it all to the table…as much as I want… for as long as I want…until I want no more. You put me to sleep then you cuddle me in those big strong arms of yours. Damn right, I love you and those dirty draws of yours too!

I cater to you...I cook your meals, clean your clothes, massage your pain away. I anticipate your needs before you ask. After a long day of work, I have a hot bath drawn just the way you like with a tad of Epsom Salt and a spoonful of bubbles. I add a few candles for the ambiance and bring you your favorite drink… even if it's me you thirst for. Some women may call me crazy and stuck in another time zone but that's okay. If loving you is played out, I don't want to be current. I like seeing your face before I close my eyes at night and when I open them in the morning. I like the security that comes with trusting you. I like the way you take care of our home. Yes, baby I love your dirty draws and will continue to wash, dry, iron, fold and put them away.

All Yours!

Dear,

Let's get away! Somewhere far from this chaos we've become accustomed to. This ain't living! Let's go somewhere fun. Where we can ride bikes, paddle board, roller skate, drive old cars, and fly kites. Let's get gone! I'll pack a small bag complete with toothbrushes, credit cards and underwear. We need to go where we can breathe new air. Where strangers smile as they pass by. Let's get away so that we can come together.

I'm sick of the tock of the clock. It reminds me of moments lost. And the awful creaks and cracks of settling into the morose side of life. Enough. Darling, I'm afraid if we don't get to moving now we'll run out of time. I filled up the tank with gas on my home...let's go!

Been Ready

Honey,

Hurry home! I've been planning something special for you all day. Don't make any stops on your way in. If your boss asks you to do overtime, tell her your woman said, "Not this time!" Hurry home darling. I've got something waiting for you. I don't need anything from the grocery store, not one single thing. The kids are fine. My sister picked them up for the weekend about an hour ago.

Hurry home, my darling! I have your bath water nice and hot just the way you like it. I bought this special oil that I'm going to rub you down in. I picked up a few of our favorite dishes from our favorite restaurant.

Hurry home, my love, while everything's HOT!

Waiting,

Your Lover

Baby,

I just want to say that I'm aware that I need to do better by you. I know that I take you for granted more times than not. Always complaining of being too tired to cook and make love to you. I've noticed lately that you no longer ask for those things. I must admit that I've became too comfortable in the arms of your stability. You got my attention the other day. After work you showered, dressed then went back out to have a few drinks with "friends."

Baby that was my cue that it was time to up my game. So, I met you at the door scantily dressed. We made love all night then took off from work the next day to finish what we'd started. I almost forgot how good you were. Assured that you were satisfied I served you your favorite breakfast in bed. Blueberry pancakes, bacon and a hot cup of black coffee, no cream. I picked up the kids and let you rest.

Darling, I knew if I continued to take you for granted I would lose you. You are the beat of my heart and without you I would be incomplete.

Love,

Your Wife

Darling,

I'm sitting here thinking about our first date. I still can't get over how much fun we had. It was like we'd known each other a long time. The chemistry between us was amazing, almost too good to be true. You kept telling me to relax and go with the flow. Now here we are three years later and about to walk down the aisle. Who knew?

Everywhere I look I see your reflection. I smell you. I can't get enough of you. You are still amazed at how I am head-over-heels in love with you. It's easy because you are safe. Soon we'll be making a vow to walk through life hand-in-hand for the rest of our days. You are my answered prayer in the flesh.

When my dad passed away I prayed that God would send me a man that cherished me as much as my father did. God gave me you and exceeded my expectations.

May God continue to bless our love into eternity.

Love,

Your Fiancé

Dear Son,

I need to apologize to you for creating so much confusion in your life. I never thought I'd be the mom who'd get involved in her son's romantic relationships, telling him who he should or shouldn't date. Even to the point of demanding to meet your girlfriends only to offer my disapproval of them. They could never be good enough for you…for me. I almost lost you, son, and that terrified me because I would have lost the opportunity to be in my grandchildren's lives.

I don't know when I crossed the line or if there was ever a line to cross. It was more of a cord, the maternal cord that connected you to me upon your inception. You were my dream come true, my reason for living. My concern for you turned into controlling behaviors that you let play out because you never wanted to hurt me. I took every chance I could to remind you of the sacrifices I made on your behalf.

I knew how to guilt you into accommodating me. To the detriment of us both this scheme of mine worked for many years. You were teased for being a "Momma's Boy" and I was accused of being too controlling of you. Son, I apologize for using your love against you. So now I release you to be the man that God always wanted you to become. As I understand that being your mother doesn't give me ownership of you. Please forgive me son.

Mom

Honey,

I love the way you handle your business. You don't have any hang ups about me earning more money than you. What's mine is yours and what's yours is mine. My only desire is to build you up to where you are trying to go. I don't mind being the breadwinner while you attend college full time. Darling, I got you. It's actually nice having you home during the day because it saves us a lot of money on childcare. You've spoiled me and the kids with daily home cooked meals. Your contributions to the household go well beyond money. I love you and will continue to support you in any way I can.

Love,

Your Woman

My Sweet I love you!

I know I say it often but I wanted to take the time to explain what it is exactly that I love about you. Let me first start with your eyes, they are like deep, deep waters. I cannot look into them without being drawn in. Those lips of yours could melt the ice off the hardest of hearts. If you'd let me, I would kiss you all night. I love the strength of your arms, they know how to hold onto what's important.

Let's see, what else do I love about you? Oh, I love how committed you are to our family. Your presence screams even when you're silent. That's the other thing, when you speak you have something to say. Sometimes I just sit and watch you staring off into the distance. You'll be in such deep thought that you don't seem to notice I'm there. You told me it was doing those times that you were praying. My God! I love that you love God.

There's more...I love how you treat your mom. You are always there for her. Whether it's picking up her groceries, fixing things around the house or inviting her over for Sunday dinner. Even still you've made it clear that I too am your priority. Baby, do you know how good it feels not to have to compete for your love? You've established clear boundaries with your mother concerning your wife.

This may be too much information for others to hear, but I have to let you know how much I love the way you've studied my body. You know me inside out.

Continued…

You make sure that I'm satisfied, I mean full! I love that I get to say that you are my man, my husband, the father of my children. Just as important, you are my friend.

Love,

Your Wife

Babe,

I know we're on this roller coaster ride called life where everything is for sale yet of little value. But despite the chaos around us we've managed to create something magical. It's in our love where I feel safe. I feel safe because I know that you say what you mean and you mean what you say. As much as you let me have my way there are times when you have to draw the line and stand for what's in the best interest of our love. Although I get mad at you, I have mad respect for you because you give me what I don't always know I need. You read me. You bring out my best, I get pleasure out of satisfying you and tasting all your chocolate flavors. Dark chocolate is my favorite!

When I dip my cookies into you what a delicious treat! Babe, we made this, we worked for this and we can have it for as long as we want. Waking up to your love nothing seems impossible. Our love has stood the test of time and sometimes the seductive one will pop in to see if we're tired and want "something" different. But we're smart enough to know the grass don't get no greener than this.

Grateful,

Your Wife

Son,

Please forgive me for keeping your father away! You needed him in ways that I could never have imagined. I thought I could be everything that you needed but, I am not a man. I called myself shielding you from the dangers of the street only to have you bring the streets into my home. Now I find myself wondering where I went wrong. Was it when I showered you with expensive gifts asking only that you focused your attention on finishing school? Or when I decided to slack up on giving you responsibilities because I thought school was enough for you to contend with? It seemed the older you became the harder it was for me to correct you. I can't get you to do anything around the house without threatening to kick your ass or kiss it!

When I began to see that you lacked motivation to make something of your life I blamed myself for that too. Regretting the times when I broke your falls because now you don't have a clue what it means to work hard and be accountable for your decisions. But, my dear son, the day has finally arrived when you have to learn. There's no easy way to say this so here it is…you have four months to get yourself together and find somewhere else to live.

Mother

Baby,

I want a real love...that sweet funky sensation! I want an audience of two, just me and you. Other people's opinions and unsolicited advice are not welcomed. I want the kind of love that hurts so good. The love that makes me call out for Daddy because I know he isn't coming! I want you to think of me throughout your day. I want to be your relief. Yes, I want it all and I want to give my all to you. A place where we can WE, yet you can be you and I can be me.

Will you be my love and love me gently into the night? Will you love me the way I want to be loved, forgetting everything that you left behind? Will you make it a priority to satisfy me? Will you? Will you do that for me?

Love,

Your Sweet

Please Baby Please,

I need you to squeeze my pain away. Rock me in your strength and make love to my heart...over and over again! In this moment, I want everything you've got. Your protection. Your passion. Your love. The covering. I need you beside me to walk this journey called life. With you by my side I know that I'll be ok, come what may.

Your Lady

Dear Lover,

I'm so sorry for how I treated you while I was trying to learn who I was. I was a mess! Forever changing my mind about our love, yanking your heart strings as if they weren't connected to your soul. One minute I was sharing my dreams of our future then the next I was pulling it all down with the same tongue. It's difficult to admit but I was afraid of letting go in our love. The vulnerability was terrifying! I didn't want to lose myself. I couldn't give in to you and hold on to me. So I chose me. Yet, here I am years later all the wiser constantly reminded of what could have been.

It's not that I planned it but I went into a period of abstinence and solitude. I knew that if I was going to change I had to learn to love myself, while exploring my fear of being vulnerable. I had to look my past in the face and proclaim that it could no longer hold me captive in fear. Today, I understand my power as a woman. I want to build my man up not tear him down. I'm forty-seven years old and I have never given my whole heart to anyone. The next man that comes along will get all of me. Who knows? Maybe you'll be that one.

Sincerely,

Toni

Epilogue

Dear Mr. President

This book would be incomplete without honoring you for the office you hold and the integrity with which you've upheld it. I, like so many others in this country and abroad, were overwhelmed with joy, hope and fear when you were elected as the 44th President of the United States. You made history when you took up residence at 1600 Pennsylvania Avenue.

I can remember the night you became President of the United States. I was driving home when I heard the radio announcer say, "Its official...Barack Obama has been elected the President of the United States!" I could barely see through my tears as I called my childhood girlfriend screaming, "He did it! He did! Hallelujah! Then we cried together celebrating the fact that a black man had finally become the President of the United States. I even wept for the ancestors who didn't believe that moment was possible. I stood as a witness that God kept his promise. I remembered being full of promise during the days that followed.

Change had come to America but not everyone was ready. Many were satisfied with the privileges bestowed upon them by the status quo. I watched as the honeymoon of your office was abruptly terminated. Mr. President did you understand that you would be immersed in the annals of spiritual wickedness in high places? Did you understand that the first has it worst?

Continued...

Mr. President, the one fact that gave me solace as I watched you walk through the Valley of the shadows of Death was that I knew you were a praying man surrounded by a praying wife and family. There were Angels appointed to watch over you.

So instead of fearing for your safety I thanked God for keeping you. Surely your road to and through the White House hasn't been easy but some black man had to say, "Here I am Lord, use me."

People can say whatever they want about you, but they'll never be able to change that fact that you Barack Hussein Obama is the 44th President of the United States with all the privileges that go with that!

Thank you for your service to this country. May God continue to bless you and yours!

Best!

Toni Cole

GOD KNOWS

Now…I said to the man who stood at the gate of the year:

"Give me a light that I may tread safely into the unknown."

And he replied:

"Go out into the darkness and put your hand into the hand of GOD. That shall be to you better that light and safer than a known way."

Minnie Louise Haskins (1875-1957)

www.ingramcontent.com/pod-product-compliance
Lightning Source LLC
Chambersburg PA
CBHW051708090426
42736CB00013B/2592